SINGLENESS
How to Be Single & Satisfied

JUNE HUNT

AspirePress

Torrance, California

Singleness: How to Be Single & Satisfied
Copyright © 2014 Hope For The Heart
All rights reserved.
Aspire Press, a division of Rose Publishing, Inc.
4733 Torrance Blvd., #259
Torrance, California 90503 USA
www.aspirepress.com

Register your book at www.aspirepress.com/register
Get inspiration via email, sign up at www.aspirepress.com

Printed in the United States of America
010114DP

CONTENTS

Dear Single Friend,

I can't begin to count the times I've been asked, "Why are you *still* single?"

Over the years, one of my stock answers has been, "I don't think of myself as 'being single'—I'm just an unclaimed blessing!" (My light-hearted response always brings a smile!)

Actually, I've recognized that some married folks have felt uncomfortable with my unmarried status. They've made comments like, "Bless your heart. I'm so sorry you don't have a husband. One day, Mr. Right will come along and complete you."

The problem with this mind-set is its implication: I'm not a *whole* person. I'm merely a fraction. I'm half a person. I have to have a mate to make me "whole."

Well, I waited for Mr. Right to appear at my doorstep ... but he never showed up! Now let's get real: I am "one" person and *one is a whole number*! I don't need anyone to complete me, because the Bible says I am *"complete in Him* [Christ]" (Colossians 2:10 NKJV).

So many singles obsess over what they think they are missing. However, I remember reading about a "spinster" named Harriet Hartbyrne who died at age 87. In her last will and testament, she said, "I don't want anybody to put 'Miss' on my tombstone. I haven't missed as much as some people think!"

The fact is, Jesus was single—and He didn't need someone to complete Him. The apostle Paul was single—and he didn't need someone to complete him. Regardless of your marital status—you don't need someone to complete you.

When you realize this truth, then for whatever time you are single, your sovereign God plans to use you as a single person in a positive way according to His plan. Englishman Charles Haddon Spurgeon—the most renowned theologian of the 19th century—once said, "Had any other condition been better for you than the one in which you find yourself, divine love would have placed you there." By embracing this truth, you too can be *single and satisfied*.

Yours in the Lord's hope,

June Hunt

SINGLENESS
How to Be Single & Satisfied

He goes to weddings—always as a guest, never as the groom. He takes gifts to the bride and groom, but has not been gifted with a bride of his own. Some of his friends have established careers and nice homes. He, on the other hand, owns no home and is just beginning a new career with meager finances. When visiting his married friends, he holds their children and spends time with them. They are drawn to him, though he has no children of his own.

He is a virile man with natural sexual desires, a man who experiences true temptation. He is a man of spiritual commitment that keeps him from sexual involvement outside of marriage.

He is regarded by some in his community as different—a misfit, not conforming to society's norm. However, he is intelligent, verbally gifted, and more than able to hold his own in community debates. He is not afraid to express his thoughts and feelings publicly, not ashamed to shed a tear among friends.

He is a content, confident man who knows who he is and what he wants, yet he does experience times of intense loneliness and longing. Typically, he is not thought of in this way, but this single man's name is Jesus—Jesus the Christ, the Son of the Living God.

DEFINITIONS

Although certain sects within Judaism encouraged remaining unmarried in order to foster devotion to God, it was certainly not typical behavior in the culture into which Jesus was born more than 2,000 years ago. Yet He was not the only one who, for whatever reason, was unmarried and yet lived a fulfilled and productive life. The single life is a *special life* that offers *special opportunities* and has *special meaning* for those who choose it—or for those who choose to accept their unmarried state with contentment. As the apostle Paul said about his singleness ...

> "I wish that all men were as I am.
> But each man has his own gift from God;
> one has this gift, another has that."
> (1 Corinthians 7:7)

WHAT DOES It Mean to Be Single?

Single, successful, and satisfied. Lydia is a prominent businesswoman—her customers value her fabrics, specifically the ones with rich purple hues. And because she is totally devoted to God, she regularly goes to a place of prayer on a riverbank outside the city. One day at that special place, her life is changed forever.

On this day her routine is interrupted by the appearance of two men. As they share the story of Jesus—presenting Him as the long-awaited Messiah—Lydia's heart responds to their message, and she receives Jesus as her Lord and Savior. That very day she is baptized, along with other members of her family.

Lydia then invites these two guests to stay in her home, and they do. This is the first of many visits.

In fact, on one occasion these two influential men—Paul and Silas—are imprisoned for their faith. Upon their release, they meet with other believers at Lydia's house, the location of the first church in Philippi. Lydia epitomizes the heart and focus of the single woman that Paul describes in 1 Corinthians 7:34. She is *"concerned about the Lord's affairs: Her aim is to be devoted to the Lord in both body and spirit."*

▶ *Single* means "a separate, unique whole"—an unbroken, undivided individual.[1]

▶ *Single* suggests being exclusively attentive:

- "single-minded" as having one aim or purpose
- "single-hearted" as having sincerity of heart and purpose or being honest and straight-forward
- "single handed" as having performed a task alone or unassisted[2]

▶ *Single* comes from the Latin word *singulus*, which means "one only."

> "The entire law is summed up
> in a single command: 'Love your
> neighbor as yourself.'"
> (Galatians 5:14)

WHAT IS Singleness?

Anna had been graced by the Spirit of God to be a prophetess for Israel. After only seven years of marriage, Anna's husband died. She then devoted the rest of her years to serving the Lord and lived to be at least 84 years old. What an excellent use of her singleness! The crowning moment of her life occurred as she witnessed the presentation of the infant Jesus at the temple. At that moment, she praised God and proclaimed to all that He was, indeed, the long-awaited Messiah.

> "Coming up to them at that very moment,
> she gave thanks to God and spoke about
> the child to all who were looking forward
> to the redemption of Jerusalem."
> (Luke 2:38)

▶ *Singleness* is the state of any man or woman of marriageable age who is not married. The Bible speaks of Philip the evangelist with "*four unmarried daughters*" who had the gift of prophecy.

"He had four unmarried daughters who prophesied." (Acts 21:9)

▶ *Single*, which refers to the state of being "unmarried or unwed,"[3] is a translation of the Greek word *agamos*. This word is used four times in 1 Corinthians 7, primarily to encourage the unmarried to remain unmarried.

▶ *Singleness* is a term that includes three categories of single adults, each with unique areas of concern, but all with similar challenges:

1. **Single for All Seasons**—Adults who never marry

2. **Single for a Season**—Adults who will marry sometime in the future

3. **Single Again**

    ▶ The widowed whose mates have died

    ▶ The divorced whose marriage contracts are terminated

    ▶ The separated who are technically married, but not living with their mates because one is ...

      ▪ away serving in the military

      ▪ away because of serving time in prison

      ▪ away because of out-of-town employment

      ▪ away because of desertion, abuse, or unresolved conflicts

"May the LORD keep watch between you and me when we are away from each other." (Genesis 31:49)

Although single people are unmarried for various reasons, how they respond to their single state is all important. Some singles, like Anna, who was widowed at a young age, choose to remain single and give their lives to serving the Lord, while other singles choose to remarry—with God's blessing. The apostle Paul makes this statement,

> "To the unmarried and the widows
> I say: It is good for them
> to stay unmarried, as I am."
> (1 Corinthians 7:8)

WHAT ARE Myths about Singleness?

Myths about singleness abound, and the assumption is often that those who are single are "second class." But look at the extraordinary life of John the Baptist. The Bible never mentions the marital status of John the Baptist. However, his ascetic lifestyle indicates a life of singleness. His calling from God requires him to prepare the way for the coming Messiah. As a result, he calls a nation to repentance, stands against evil kings, and dies a martyr's death. Jesus Himself proclaimed,

> "I tell you, among those born of women
> there is no one greater than John."
> (Luke 7:28)

Myth of the Never Married

▶ **Myth:** "God's *best* is marriage. Singleness is *second* best."

Truth: According to Scripture, marriage is best for those God calls to be married, and singleness is best for those God calls to be single. Singleness is referred to as the best state for having undivided devotion to the Lord.

"Are you unmarried? Do not look for a wife. ... I am saying this for your own good, not to restrict you, but that you may live in a right way in undivided devotion to the Lord." (1 Corinthians 7:27, 35)

Myth of the Separated

▶ **Myth:** "Living in limbo is terrible. *Any* decision is better than *no* decision."

Truth: God wants us to learn to be content in any state and to patiently wait on His timing.

"I have learned to be content whatever the circumstances." (Philippians 4:11)

Myth of the Divorced

▶ **Myth:** "All you need is another mate. Then you will find fulfillment again."

Truth: Contentment and fulfillment are found in relationship with the Lord, who is always with you.

"Be content with what you have, because God has said, 'Never will I leave you; never will I forsake you.'" (Hebrews 13:5)

Myth of the Widowed

▶ **Myth:** "After your mate dies, you are left incomplete and unfulfilled."

Truth: You will grieve the loss of your spouse deeply, but as a Christian, you are given complete fullness in Christ, whether married or single.

"You are complete in Him [Christ].*"*
(Colossians 2:10 NKJV)

Myth of the State of Singleness

▶ **Myth:** "Since God uses the family to build character, you will never become mature if you remain unmarried."[4]

Truth: Your marital state does not determine the degree of your maturity. When you become a believer, God takes the responsibility to bring you to maturity.

"He who began a good work in you will carry it on to completion." (Philippians 1:6)

CHARACTERISTICS OF THOSE WHO ARE SINGLE

Elijah is one of the most powerful prophets of the Old Testament, but at one point he finds himself on the run from a powerful queen. Elijah is single and has single-handedly won a showdown with 450 false prophets on Mount Carmel. The prophets of Baal wail for hours for their god to send fire from on high, but to no avail. Then Elijah voices a short, two-sentence prayer to the only true God, who responds by raining down fire from heaven.

Elijah then rids the land of every false prophet. For that, the evil Queen Jezebel vows to take vengeance upon him before another day passes. With a death contract over his head, Elijah runs for his life. Exhausted, he arrives in the Negev Desert and desires to die. *"I have had enough, LORD. ... Take my life"* (1 Kings 19:4).

Imagine: here is victorious Elijah—despondent, discouraged, depressed—and in absolute despair. But God Himself ministers to Elijah, providing food and drink through the angel of the Lord. Still continuing to run away, Elijah then travels 40 days and 40 nights until he reaches Mount Horeb. There, Elijah has another encounter with the living God and laments that he is totally alone: *"The Israelites have rejected your covenant, broken down your altars, and put your prophets to death with the sword. I am the only one left, and now they are trying to kill me too"* (1 Kings 19:10).

The Lord, however, encourages Elijah by telling him there are 7,000 in Israel whom He has reserved—7,000 who have remained faithful. *"I reserve seven thousand in Israel—all whose knees have not bowed down to Baal and all whose mouths have not kissed him"* (1 Kings 19:18).

WHAT ARE Difficulties in Living as a Single?[5]

Singles today need reassurance from God that, like Elijah, they are not really alone, not abandoned, not lost among the throngs. Although singleness in itself is to be considered a blessing, it can bring with it perplexing, yet solvable burdens, as evidenced by the fact that *"Elijah was afraid and ran for his life"* (1 Kings 19:3).

So often, those who struggle with their singleness have questions revolving around the five "W"s and an "H": *who*, *where*, *what*, *why*, *when*, and *how*.

▶ **Difficulty with Self-Image**

Faced with the threat of death, Elijah wanted to die. Like Elijah, at times have you forgotten who you are, and how God sees you?

Common questions when you struggle with your self-image:

- "*Who* am I?"
- "*Where* do I belong?"
- "*What* is my purpose?"
- "*Why* am I here?"
- "*When* will I find fulfillment?"
- "*How* can I find direction for my life?"

The answer from the Bible is ...

"We are God's workmanship, created in Christ Jesus to do good works, which God prepared in advance for us to do." (Ephesians 2:10)

▶ **Difficulty with Loneliness**

The name *Elijah* means "Jehovah is my God." As it turned out, 7,000 others also acknowledged Jehovah as God. Like Elijah, have you at times found yourself feeling desperately destitute and desperately lonely?

Common questions when you feel lonely:

- "*Who* can I share my life with?"
- "*Where* will I go when I need help?"
- "*What* will I do when I get sick?"
- "*Why* do I keep feeling so alone?"
- "*When* can I have fulfilling companionship?"
- "*How* will I make it emotionally and financially on my own?"

The answer from the Bible is ...

"The LORD himself goes before you and will be with you; he will never leave you nor forsake you. Do not be afraid; do not be discouraged." (Deuteronomy 31:8)

▶ Difficulty with Rejection

Elijah felt completely rejected by his countrymen, assuming no one was on his side, thus he completely cut himself off from everyone. Like Elijah, at times have you felt so rejected that you tried to cut yourself off from everyone?

Common questions when you feel rejected:

- *"Who* will love me unconditionally?"
- *"Where* will I find true acceptance?"
- *"What* is wrong with me?"
- *"Why* do I feel like a second-class citizen?"
- *"When* will my desire to have a family be fulfilled or disappear?"
- *"How* can I keep from feeling unwanted?"

The answer from the Bible is ...

"How great is the love the Father has lavished on us, that we should be called children of God!" (1 John 3:1)

▶ Difficulty with Self-Worth

Obviously, Elijah's self-worth went from a ten to a zero in the span of one day. He had soundly triumphed over the false prophets but was then thoroughly terrorized by the enemy queen. Like

Elijah, at times have you faced such opposition that you felt you had little worth?

Common questions when you feel worthless:

- "*Who* will make me feel important?"
- "*Where* will I find affirmation?"
- "*What* makes me valuable?"
- "*Why* am I not worthy enough to be loved?"
- "*When* will I find meaning and purpose in my life?"
- "*How* can I know my worth?"

The answer from the Bible is ...

"You are precious and honored in my sight." (Isaiah 43:4)

WHAT THREE STRUGGLES Do Discontented Singles Share?

The pressure can really mount—the pressure to *marry*.

But *singleness* is neither inferior to nor superior to marriage. However, in a society where people often walk in pairs, some singles focus on what they *don't* have and therefore may struggle with their sexuality, develop a bondage to bitterness, or consistently fight with their fears.

▶ The Struggle with Sexuality

Common questions when you feel sexually unfulfilled:

- "How can I ignore my sexuality?"
- "How should I deal with my sexual desires?"
- "How do I handle my feeling that I'm missing out on sexual fulfillment?"
- "How do I respond to others who see me as sexually defective?"
- "How could God make me a sexual being and then deny me a sexual relationship?"
- "How am I to express my sexuality outside of marriage?"

The Bible says ...

"Offer your bodies as living sacrifices, holy and pleasing to God—this is your spiritual act of worship." (Romans 12:1)

▶ The Bondage of Bitterness

Common questions when you feel bitter:

- "Why am I not receiving the best in life?"
- "Why is God punishing me?"
- "Why doesn't God care about my needs and desires?"
- "Why would I trust a God who would leave me all alone?"
- "Why do others deserve a happy marriage and I don't?"
- "Why is life so unfair?"

The Bible says ...

"See to it that no one misses the grace of God and that no bitter root grows up to cause trouble and defile many." (Hebrews 12:15)

▶ The Fight with Fear

Common questions when you feel fearful:

- "Will I always feel like I'm missing out on life?"
- "Will I be safe living alone?"
- "Will someone protect me from being hurt by others?"
- "Will I be all alone when I am old?"
- "Will I become incapacitated and have no one to care for me?"
- "Will I have someone to turn to in a crisis?"

The Bible says ...

"Do not fear, for I am with you; do not be dismayed, for I am your God. I will strengthen you and help you; I will uphold you with my righteous right hand." (Isaiah 41:10)

John Calvin, the doctor of Geneva and chief theologian of the Reformation, was one of the most significant Christian thinkers in all of history. Like Jesus, he went against the grain of religious leaders. And like Jesus, he made significant contributions to virtually every area of Christian theology. His many volumes of writing include the *Institutes of the Christian Religion*.

Calvin lost his wife after only nine years of marriage, and they had endured the death of their only son in infancy. Following his wife's death, Calvin remained unmarried for the final years of his life and ministry. These words from the apostle Paul could certainly be applied to the dedicated life of John Calvin—one of the greatest spiritual teachers—who was content to remain a single widower.

> "Because of the service by which
> you have proved yourselves,
> men will praise God for the obedience that
> accompanies your confession of the gospel
> of Christ, and for your generosity in sharing
> with them and with everyone else."
> (2 Corinthians 9:13)

The Contentment Checklist

Not every single person will relate to each of the following statements, but the more content you are with your singleness, the more these statements will be true for you.

Personal Contentment

☐ I enjoy being single.

☐ I consider myself a joyful person—I am not looking for a mate to make me happy.

☐ I know and appreciate the benefits of being single.

☐ I appreciate the freedom to spontaneously make plans and go places.

☐ I am a whole person within myself—I'm not looking for a mate to complete me.

☐ I am grateful for what I have in my life—I do not dwell on what I don't have.

☐ I am content when I spend time alone.

☐ I am often alone, but rarely do I feel lonely.

☐ I like being able to choose when to be alone and when to be with others.

☐ I am not resentful or morose that I am unmarried.

☐ I don't fear negative words from others about my singleness.

☐ I am at peace as a single person.

"A heart at peace gives life to the body,
but envy rots the bones."
(Proverbs 14:30)

Social Contentment

☐ I am comfortable going to social gatherings with others or alone.

☐ I can enjoy my friends of the opposite sex without looking at them as potential mates.

☐ I can attend weddings without feeling sorry for myself.

☐ I do not envy married couples.

☐ I am building close, fulfilling relationships with family members and friends.

☐ I am investing in the lives of my nieces and nephews and/or other young people.

☐ I enjoy gathering with my friends for times of fellowship.

☐ I enjoy nurturing several healthy friendships—not just one.

☐ I initiate activities with others instead of waiting for others to reach out to me.

☐ I find joy in serving others through the gifts God has given me.

☐ I enjoy the camaraderie of both single and married friends.

☐ I have a "family of friends" with whom I am open and honest about my personal trials and temptations and to whom I am accountable.

"As iron sharpens iron,
so one man sharpens another."
(Proverbs 27:17)

24

Spiritual Contentment

- ☐ I consider singleness a state blessed by God.

- ☐ I have found my significance and security in the Lord.

- ☐ I am developing a more intimate relationship with the Lord.

- ☐ I depend on the Lord to give my life meaning and purpose.

- ☐ I have made it my goal to be the person God created me to be.

- ☐ I am involved in a meaningful, group Bible study.

- ☐ I enjoy being an active part of my church.

- ☐ I focus on whom the Lord has put in my life.

- ☐ I have developed a "spiritual family" to whom I am accountable.

- ☐ I trust the Lord with His plans for my life.

- ☐ I love the Lord with all my heart, mind, soul, and strength.

- ☐ I delight in praying to and praising the Lord.

"Praise the LORD, O my soul;
all my inmost being, praise his holy name.
Praise the LORD, O my soul,
and forget not all his benefits."
(Psalm 103:1–2)

QUESTION: "Is it scriptural to participate in matchmaking services?"

ANSWER: Since the 1990s, online dating and face-to-face subscription dating services have mushroomed in popularity among non-Christians and Christians alike. As with any major decision that relies on judgment and integrity, a decision to use dating services should be approached with great caution and care—and great prayer. Opportunities abound for fraud, and the ability to get to know others is only as effective as their willingness to reveal their true, authentic selves. Before you decide to participate in a dating service, examine yourself.

- What are your motives?
- What are your goals?
- Do you have a contented spirit?
- Do you have the peace of God?
- Will you involve your Christian "community" in your online dating decision and experience?

Always remember, God is your source. A dating service is not. Scripture says ...

"Whether you turn to the right or to the left, your ears will hear a voice behind you, saying, 'This is the way; walk in it.'"
(Isaiah 30:21)

CAUSES OF SINGLENESS AND DISCONTENTMENT AMONG SINGLES

Singles are unmarried for various reasons. And for various reasons some who are unmarried are perfectly content and others are not. Of course, the same can be said of those who are married. But what are reasons some people remain single and satisfied, and what are reasons for discontentment among some singles?

Two women who illustrate this contrast are mentioned in the Bible:

▶ **Dorcas** didn't have time to wring her hands over widowhood because she kept them too busy serving others.

▶ **Naomi**, on the other hand, spent too much time languishing over her loneliness and loss.

They are two women in the same situation, each with a different response to singleness and God's call on their lives. In time, both will experience His miraculous hand at work and both will receive honor.

And for both, the words for widows spoken by the apostle Paul prove to be absolutely accurate:

"A woman is bound to her husband as long as he lives. But if her husband dies, she is

free to marry anyone she wishes, but he must belong to the Lord. In my judgment, she is happier if she stays as she is—and I think that I too have the Spirit of God."
(1 Corinthians 7:39–40)

WHY DO So Many Choose Singleness?[6]

Dorcas was a disciple in Joppa and was known for *"always doing good and helping the poor."* She was beloved by all those around her. But tragedy struck when Dorcas became ill and died, prompting tearful laments—*and actions*—from those feeling their immense loss.

Two men sent for Peter and urged him, *"Please come at once!"* Upon arrival, Peter immediately saw the fruit of Dorcas' faithfulness. Numerous widows encircled him, crying and holding up robes and other types of clothing she had made. Clearly, Dorcas had used her singleness as a springboard for service to those around her. In the midst of her singleness, she chose to be single-minded—not focusing on herself and her own needs—but focusing on God's plan to use her in meeting the needs of others.

Peter then asked everyone to leave the room where Dorcas lay lifeless. After he knelt and prayed, he told Dorcas to get up, whereupon *"she opened her eyes, and seeing Peter she sat up"* (Acts 9:36–40).

Immediately, Dorcas was presented alive to her astonished mourners. Undoubtedly, her charitable ministry continued, and God greatly used her singleness in her ministry.

WHY SELECT SINGLENESS?

▶ **Some decide to postpone marriage because ...**

- They want to travel and see the world.
- They are in training programs or postgraduate work.
- They are beginning medical school or military service.
- They have jobs requiring extensive travel.
- They are just starting out in the business world or other careers.
- They want to enjoy their freedom before settling down.
- They are still grieving the death of a mate.
- They want to focus on raising their children.
- They have not found a suitable mate yet.
- They want to "try out" cohabitation to see if they really get along well.

▶ **Some decide not to marry because ...**

- They feel called by God to singleness.
- They believe marriage would hinder their ministry to others.
- They feel married to their careers and/or ministries.

- They prefer the freedoms of singleness over the restrictions of marriage.
- They do not want the responsibilities of marriage.
- They have a severe illness or handicap that influences their decision.
- They do not feel drawn to the opposite sex in a marital way.
- They have negative views of the opposite sex as a result of abuse.
- They have parents who were unhappily married.
- They are struggling with gender identity issues.
- They had marriages end in painful divorce.
- They have difficulty making a commitment.
- They have been rejected and won't risk further rejection.

Ultimately, only God knows what will fulfill His purpose for your life and, as a result, will give you the greatest fulfillment. If you really want God's best, pray for His perfect will.

> "I desire to do your will, O my God;
> your law is within my heart."
> (Psalm 40:8)

It was the common custom of the day—it was the prevailing practice.

The typical family tradition required the eldest daughter to be the first given in marriage.

The Bible explains that Jacob, however, loved *second-born* Rachel. So he made an arrangement with her father, Laban, to work seven years for her hand in marriage.

If you were the eldest daughter, imagine the pressure to marry—especially if a suitor wanted to marry your younger sister.

Imagine what it would be like to be Jacob, who works seven years for the right to marry beautiful Rachel, and then in the darkness of the wedding night he unknowingly sleeps with Leah. What a deception concocted by his new father-in-law! Now Jacob is forced to work another seven years for the hand of his beloved Rachel.

PRESSURE! PRESSURE! PRESSURE!

And pressure continues today—in different cultures, over different issues, within different families, among different friends.

▶ Parental Pressure

- Parents who assume marriage is your only route to happiness
- Parents who want a son-in-law or daughter-in-law
- Parents who want you to have the love of a "soul mate"
- Parents who want grandchildren
- Parents who desire a secure future for you
- Parents who don't want you to be alone

"Fathers, do not exasperate your children; instead, bring them up in the training and instruction of the Lord." (Ephesians 6:4)

▶ Peer Pressure

- Friends who want you to "fit in"
- Friends who want you to be like them
- Friends who push you to make a commitment
- Friends who view you as unfulfilled
- Friends who seek to be your "matchmaker"
- Friends who think you would be an ideal mate for someone

Paul's friends pressured him not to go to Jerusalem, but Luke writes, *"When he would not be dissuaded, we gave up and said, 'The Lord's will be done'"* (Acts 21:14).

▶ Professional Pressure

- Professions in which you are expected to be married
- Professions that cater to married couples
- Professionals who view a married employee as more stable and dependable
- Professionals who consider singles a threat
- Professional organizations that place singles in a "second class status"

"If you show favoritism, you sin and are convicted by the law as lawbreakers." (James 2:9)

▶ Personal Pressure

- Personally desiring children
- Personally desiring a sexual relationship or partner
- Personally fearing financial insecurity
- Personally experiencing difficulties in getting credit, insurance, or loans
- Personally paying income taxes at higher rates
- Personally desiring a home—somewhere to belong and someone to belong to

"Do nothing out of selfish ambition or vain conceit, but in humility consider others better than yourselves." (Philippians 2:3)

Naomi returns to her hometown with daughter-in-law Ruth by her side, but the three people who had left with her many years before are noticeably absent ... and the whole town is astir.

"Can this be Naomi?" the women exclaim, probably stretching their necks to see whether her husband and two sons are following far behind. But no, each one has died.

The widow Naomi becomes embittered by her circumstances and wants her name to reflect her bitter anguish. *"'Don't call me Naomi,' she told them. 'Call me Mara, because the Almighty has made my life very bitter. I went away full, but the LORD has brought me back empty. Why call me Naomi? The LORD has afflicted me; the Almighty has brought misfortune upon me'"* (Ruth 1:19–21).

Naomi, Mara—the two names had distinctly different meanings, which clearly conveyed the woeful woman's message. *Naomi* means "pleasant," and *Mara* means "bitter." *Mara* seemed far more appropriate to Naomi since her husband and sons died while they were all living in Moab. According to her own words, she considered her life empty. She felt that her unwanted singleness was a misfortune—an affliction from God.

The root cause of discontent among singles is the unrealistic expectation that marriage and sexual expression are necessary to meet God-given inner needs for love, significance, and security. Such an expectation results in disappointment, but trusting in God alone to meet these needs leads to contentment.[7]

The Need for Unconditional Love

▶ WRONG BELIEF:

"I need to be married to feel completely loved."

RIGHT BELIEF:

"I realize that no human being can love me perfectly. I will rely on God's perfect, unconditional, and everlasting love. I will find my wholeness in Him and trust Him to make me a channel of His love to others."

"The LORD appeared to us in the past, saying: 'I have loved you with an everlasting love; I have drawn you with loving-kindness.'" (Jeremiah 31:3)

The Need for Significance

▶ WRONG BELIEF:

"I need to be married in order for my life to have significance—for there to be meaning and purpose in my life."

RIGHT BELIEF:

"Only as I more deeply understand God's purpose for me, and I embrace His purpose— will my character be conformed to the character of Christ and will I experience significance and find fulfillment."

"Those God foreknew he also predestined to be conformed to the likeness of his Son." (Romans 8:29)

The Need for Security

▶ **WRONG BELIEF:**

"I need a mate in order to feel secure."

RIGHT BELIEF:

"Security cannot be found in a person. The only lasting security is found in a close relationship with the Lord, who will never leave me nor forsake me."

"Let the beloved of the LORD rest secure in him, for he shields him all day long, and the one the LORD loves rests between his shoulders." (Deuteronomy 33:12)

Naomi's bitterness was eventually abated as she experienced the Lord's provision for her and for her beloved daughter-in-law Ruth. Once she witnessed the Lord at work in her life and perceived His plan to meet her needs and even to do the miraculous by fulfilling her dream for a grandson, her name was once again Naomi. Her life was once again "pleasant."

God did not give her another husband or more children of her own. But He gave her grandchildren through her daughter-in-law in order to carry on her family name and leave her a heritage. And how rich a heritage God gave her! Her firstborn grandson would be the grandfather of King David, through whose lineage Jesus the Christ would come. Naomi learned what everyone who is single needs to learn—that God had a divine purpose in her being single, and He has a divine purpose for your being single.

"Naomi took the child, laid him in her lap and cared for him. The women living there said, 'Naomi has a son.' And they named him Obed. He was the father of Jesse, the father of David." (Ruth 4:16–17)

Your Single Most Important Decision

The brilliant English philosopher and beloved storyteller C. S. Lewis—best known for *The Chronicles of Narnia* and *Mere Christianity*—lived most of his life as a single man and was married late in life for only four of his 65 years.

This Oxford/Cambridge professor and avowed atheist began an honest quest for truth in order to disprove Christianity. Yet, his philosophical findings became only solid proofs to confirm rather than deny the existence of God and the deity of Christ.

Ultimately, C. S. Lewis became the most respected and influential apologist of the 20th century. This atheist-turned-apologist would agree that your single most important decision is what you do with the claims of Christ.

THE FOUR POINTS YOU NEED TO KNOW

#1 God's Purpose for You is *Salvation.*

What was God's motive in sending Christ to earth?

To express His love for you by saving you!

The Bible says, *"God so loved the world that he gave his one and only Son, that whoever believes in him shall not perish but have eternal life. For God did not send his Son into the world to condemn the world, but to save the world through him."* (John 3:16–17)

What was Jesus' purpose in coming to earth?

To forgive your sins, empower you to have victory over sin, and enable you to live a fulfilled life!

Jesus said, *"I have come that they may have life, and have it to the full."* (John 10:10)

#2 Your Problem is *Sin.*

What exactly is sin?

Sin is living independently of God's standard—knowing what is right, but choosing wrong.

"Anyone, then, who knows the good he ought to do and doesn't do it, sins." (James 4:17)

What is the major consequence of sin?

Spiritual "death" which is eternal separation from God.

"Your iniquities [sins] *have separated you from your God."* (Isaiah 59:2)

"For the wages of sin is death, but the gift of God is eternal life in Christ Jesus our Lord." (Romans 6:23)

#3 God's Provision for You is the *Savior.*

Can anything remove the penalty for sin?

Yes! Jesus died on the cross to personally pay the penalty for your sins.

"God demonstrates his own love for us in this: While we were still sinners, Christ died for us." (Romans 5:8)

What is the solution to being separated from God?

Belief in (trust in) Jesus Christ as the only way to God the Father.

"Jesus answered, 'I am the way and the truth and the life. No one comes to the Father except through me.'" (John 14:6)

#4 Your Part is *Surrender.*

Give Christ control of your life—entrusting yourself to Him.

"Jesus said to his disciples, 'If anyone would come after me, he must deny himself and take up his cross [die to your own self-rule] *and follow me. For whoever wants to save his life will lose it, but whoever loses his life for me will find it. What good will it be for a man if he gains the whole world, yet forfeits his soul?'"* (Matthew 16:24–26)

Place your faith in (rely on) Jesus Christ as your personal Lord and Savior and reject your "good works" as a means of earning God's approval.

"It is by grace you have been saved, through faith—and this not from yourselves, it is the gift of God—not by works, so that no one can boast." (Ephesians 2:8–9)

The moment you choose to receive Jesus as your Lord and Savior—entrusting your life to Him—He comes to live inside you. Then He gives you His power to live the fulfilled life God has planned for you. If you want to be fully forgiven by God and become the person God created you to be, you can tell Him in a simple, heartfelt prayer like this:

PRAYER OF SALVATION

"God, I want a real relationship with You. I admit that many times I've chosen to go my own way instead of Your way. Please forgive me for my sins. Jesus, thank You for dying on the cross to pay the penalty for my sins. Come into my life to be my Lord and my Savior. Change me from the inside out and make me the person You created me to be. In Your holy name I pray. Amen."

WHAT CAN YOU EXPECT NOW?

If you sincerely prayed this prayer, look at what God says about you and your singleness.

"You are complete in Him [Christ]."
(Colossians 2:10 NKJV)

STEPS TO SOLUTION

Often the single life is deemed "second best" to what is thought to be "marital bliss," but the apostle Paul doesn't see it that way. His counsel for those longing to walk the aisle: *"It is good for them to stay unmarried, as I am"* (1 Corinthians 7:8).

Paul is not a *rebel*—just a *realist*. Singles have something unique to offer that any dutiful husband or wife cannot—*"undivided devotion to the Lord"* (1 Corinthians 7:35). Singleness can render a sharper focus to serve God.

Only one group of people can fulfill that calling with singular devotion—singles.

If a woman were married to a man whose focus was *solely* occupied with serving God, she would feel justifiable rejection and pain. Had Paul been married, his wife would have had to endure a husband who suffered greatly and was seldom at home. Paul was beaten, stoned, arrested, imprisoned, and shipwrecked in the course of ministry and was *"constantly on the move"* (2 Corinthians 11:26).

A spouse might have sidetracked and sidelined Paul, diverting his attention from the dangers of ministry to the comforts of home. But because Paul was single and singularly focused on pleasing the Lord, he could unequivocally say, *"For Christ's sake, I delight in weaknesses, in insults, in hardships, in persecutions, in difficulties"* (2 Corinthians 12:10).

Key Passage to Read

Because Paul lived effectively as a single man, he could easily speak to the issues of singles. And the most extensive section in the Bible on singleness is authored by Paul in 1 Corinthians 7.

"Context is king" is a tried and true saying and must be remembered when you seek to interpret any passage of literature accurately. Every Bible verse is written within a chapter within a book within the Old or New Testaments. It is also written within a particular time period, within a particular culture, and to a particular audience.

In order to accurately interpret the key passage here, you will need to take into consideration the context in which it was written. If you do not do this, you may get the mistaken impression that Paul was against marriage. To the contrary, Paul was conscious of the trying times and crucial circumstances in the city of Corinth, and he wanted his fellow Christians to make wise choices.

GOD'S HEART ON SINGLENESS
1 CORINTHIANS 7

▶ Singleness is a good state to be in.

"It is good for a man not to marry." (v. 1)

▶ Singleness is a gift from God.

"I wish that all men were as I am. But each man has his own gift from God; one has this gift, another has that." (v. 7)

▶ Singleness is a good state for widows.

"To the unmarried and the widows I say: It is good for them to stay unmarried, as I am." (v. 8)

▶ Singleness is the state in which to remain if separation occurs and reconciliation is impossible.

"If she does [separate], *she must remain unmarried or else be reconciled to her husband. And a husband must not divorce his wife."* (v. 11)

▶ Singles can face crises and worldly difficulties with fewer complications and less complexity.

"Because of the present crisis, I think that it is good for you to remain as you are." (v. 26)

▶ Singles should not search for mates, but seek a deeper relationship with God.

"Are you unmarried? Do not look for a wife." (v. 27)

▶ Singles face fewer troubles in life.

"If you do marry, you have not sinned; and if a virgin marries, she has not sinned. But those who marry will face many troubles in this life, and I want to spare you this." (v. 28)

▶ Singles have fewer concerns.

"I would like you to be free from concern." (v. 32)

▶ Single men can more single-mindedly focus on pleasing the Lord.

"I would like you to be free from concern. An unmarried man is concerned about the Lord's affairs—how he can please the Lord. But a married man is concerned about the affairs of this world—how he can please his wife—and his interests are divided." (vv. 32–34)

▶ Single women can more single-mindedly focus on pleasing the Lord.

"An unmarried woman or virgin is concerned about the Lord's affairs: Her aim is to be devoted to the Lord in both body and spirit. But a married woman is concerned about the affairs of this world—how she can please her husband." (v. 34)

▶ Singles can have undivided devotion to the Lord.

"I am saying this for your own good, not to restrict you, but that you may live in a right way in undivided devotion to the Lord." (v. 35)

▶ Singles have the right and the freedom to marry.

"If anyone ... feels he ought to marry, he should do as he wants. He is not sinning. They should get married." (v. 36)

▶ Singleness can be the happier state for a widow.

"She [a widow] *is happier if she stays as she is."* (v. 40)

HOW TO Choose to Be Content

Being content is admirable in anyone, but sometimes gaining and maintaining contentment in a heartbreaking situation is one of the greatest challenges faced by a single person. However, when you allow God to fulfill His purpose for your life instead of pursuing your own purposes, you unlock the door to a pathway of opportunities.

**"Godliness with contentment is great gain."
(1 Timothy 6:6)**

CONTENT

Confess the difficulty.

It is hard to give up the desires of your heart.

▶ Admit that you are discontented.

▶ Admit your anger, frustration, and loneliness.

▶ Admit your desire to marry.

▶ Admit God's right to order your life.

"I know, O LORD, that a man's life is not his own; it is not for man to direct his steps." (Jeremiah 10:23)

Overcome the "greener grass" mentality.

Don't assume that the grass is greener on the other side.

▶ Marriage does not cure loneliness.

▶ Marriage does not provide self-worth.

▶ Marriage does not cure depression.

▶ Marriage does not provide security.

"My God will meet all your needs according to his glorious riches in Christ Jesus." (Philippians 4:19)

Nourish a heart of gratefulness.

In your singleness, you can be grateful that you have the ...

▶ Freedom to be yourself, while refusing to focus on yourself exclusively

▶ Freedom to attain your own aspirations, while avoiding selfish ambition

▶ Freedom to take risks, while assuming rightful responsibilities

▶ Freedom with the use of your time, while being a good steward of your time

▶ Freedom of mobility, while still considering the needs and wishes of others

▶ Freedom in financial planning, while practicing good stewardship of your resources

▶ Freedom to nurture several deep relationships, while keeping the Lord first in your life

▶ Freedom to lean completely on the Lord, while receiving support from others

▶ Freedom to serve the Lord, while continuing to minister to the needs of others

▶ Freedom to be spontaneous, while concentrating on fulfilling your responsibilities

"Be joyful always; pray continually; give thanks in all circumstances, for this is God's will for you in Christ Jesus." (1 Thessalonians 5:16–18)

Treasure your identity in Christ.

When you give your life to Jesus Christ and His Spirit lives within you, then be assured ...

▶ You are loved.

"As the Father has loved me, so have I loved you. Now remain in my love." (John 15:9)

▶ You are totally accepted.

"Accept one another, then, just as Christ accepted you, in order to bring praise to God." (Romans 15:7)

▶ You belong to God.

"The Spirit himself testifies with our spirit that we are God's children." (Romans 8:16)

▶ You are never alone.

"The LORD himself goes before you and will be with you; he will never leave you nor forsake you. Do not be afraid; do not be discouraged." (Deuteronomy 31:8)

▶ You are free from fear.

"Cast all your anxiety on him because he cares for you." (1 Peter 5:7)

▶ You have all the confidence you need.

"The LORD will be your confidence and will keep your foot from being snared." (Proverbs 3:26)

▶ You have the mind of Christ.

"Who has known the mind of the Lord that he may instruct him? But we have the mind of Christ." (1 Corinthians 2:16)

▶ You have a purpose in life.

"The LORD will fulfill his purpose for me; your love, O LORD, endures forever." (Psalm 138:8)

▶ You have the righteousness of Christ.

"God made him who had no sin to be sin for us, so that in him we might become the righteousness of God." (2 Corinthians 5:21)

▶ You have victory over sin.

"The sting of death is sin, and the power of sin is the law. But thanks be to God! He gives us the victory through our Lord Jesus Christ." (1 Corinthians 15:56–57)

Expect God to give you a ministry.

God desires to use you in the lives of others.

▶ Learn your spiritual gift.

"Just as each of us has one body with many members, and these members do not all have the same function, so in Christ we who are many form one body, and each member belongs to all the others. We have different gifts, according to the grace given us. If a man's gift is prophesying, let him use it in proportion to his faith. If it is serving, let him serve; if it is teaching, let him teach; if it is encouraging, let him encourage; if it is contributing to the needs of others, let him give generously; if it is leadership, let him govern diligently; if it is showing mercy, let him do it cheerfully." (Romans 12:4–8)

▶ Love others with agape love (desiring another's highest good).

"Love must be sincere. Hate what is evil; cling to what is good. Be devoted to one another in brotherly love. Honor one another above yourselves. Never be lacking in zeal, but keep your spiritual fervor, serving the Lord. Be joyful in hope, patient in affliction, faithful in prayer." (Romans 12:9–12)

▶ Look for ways to meet the needs of others.

"Share with God's people who are in need. Practice hospitality. Bless those who persecute you; bless and do not curse. Rejoice with those who rejoice; mourn with those who mourn." (Romans 12:13–15)

▶ Learn the art of encouraging others.

"Live in harmony with one another. Do not be proud, but be willing to associate with people of low position. Do not be conceited. Do not repay anyone evil for evil. Be careful to do what is right in the eyes of everybody." (Romans 12:16–17)

Nurture a family of friends.

Pray for God to bring wise, faithful friends into your life.

▶ Be open to several significant relationships.

▶ Be the initiator of calls and contacts.

▶ Be consistent in planning one-on-one quality time.

▶ Be free in sharing your true thoughts and feelings.

▶ Be interested in their interests.

▶ Be compassionate about their concerns.

"A friend loves at all times." (Proverbs 17:17)

Trust your future to God.

God will meet your deepest inner needs when you lay down your life and give Him control.

▶ Lay down your emotions.

Feelings follow thinking. Place your emotions under God's authority.

▶ Lay down your thoughts.

Submit your thoughts to the Spirit's guidance. Learn to think the way God thinks through studying and memorizing Scripture.

▶ Lay down your will.

Give up having to have things your way. Give up your demands for marriage. Instead, seek His will.

▶ Lay down your expectations.

Allow the Holy Spirit to direct your aspirations.

"Seek first his kingdom and his righteousness, and all these things will be given to you as well." (Matthew 6:33)

Healthy trees are planted far apart so they can spread their roots and branches, so they can become strong as they mature. Singleness gives you space to grow. Sometimes it is harder to grow when you are too close to someone. Singleness gives you time to grow and become the person God created you to be.

Being a Healthy Single Means:

▶ Living by yourself with contentment

▶ Learning not to need a mate to make your life meaningful or complete

▶ Looking to God to satisfy the deepest needs and longings of your heart

▶ Recognizing that being married is not better, merely different

▶ Respecting *who* you are and *why* you are

▶ Realizing there will be something special "around the corner" that will benefit your life

▶ Embracing your singleness as a gift from God and as His purpose for you

▶ Enjoying the freedom to spend a week's vacation on the beach, to take computer courses, to work late on an interesting project, to spend the day with a good book or with a person who has read one

- Pursuing God rather than a marriage partner

- Feeling good about being free to make choices as God presents opportunities

- Focusing on *becoming* the right kind of person rather than *looking for* the right person

- Finding your fullness of joy in developing a more intimate relationship with God, family, and friends

HOW TO Bolster Your Self-Worth after a Broken Relationship

God created each of us with specific inner needs: the needs for love, significance, and security.[8] Typically, we look to people to meet these needs. However, God intends that we look to Him to be our Need-Meeter—with the understanding that sometimes He uses people to reinforce our sense of feeling loved, significant, and secure.

When people fail us, we can temporarily lose the sense of self-worth we had gained by having those individuals in our lives. Losing a relationship with a significant person is painful to everyone, but can be devastating for some. The remedy can be found in looking to our true Need-Meeter, to the One who gives us unfailing love, who makes us unquestionably significant, and who provides us with unshakable security.

"What a man desires is unfailing love."
(Proverbs 19:22)

LOVE

If you are feeling the void of being without a supportive relationship ...

▶ *Reject* the lie that you are unacceptable or unlovable.

Pray, "Lord, thank You that when I experience rejection, You offer me love and acceptance."

"He made us accepted in the Beloved." (Ephesians 1:6 NKJV)

▶ *Rejoice* in the truth that you are deeply loved.

Pray, "Lord, thank You for the deep, unconditional love and kindness You have for me ... that You love me even when I feel unlovable."

"I have loved you with an everlasting love; I have drawn you with loving-kindness." (Jeremiah 31:3)

▶ *Revel* in the reality that God is conforming you to the likeness of His Son!

Pray, "Lord, thank You that day by day I am becoming more and more like You. Thank You for conforming me into Your likeness."

"Those God foreknew he also predestined to be conformed to the likeness of his Son, that he might be the firstborn among many brothers." (Romans 8:29)

▶ ***Rely*** on other treasured relationships to reaffirm your value.

Pray, "Lord, I thank You for putting people in my life who value me as a person—who reaffirm that my life does have value."

"As iron sharpens iron, so one man sharpens another." (Proverbs 27:17)

▶ ***Release*** all anger, hurt, resentment, and regret to the Lord.

Pray, "Lord, thank You for taking my anger, hurt, resentment, and regret. I release it all to You and lay it all down at the foot of Your cross."

"Get rid of all bitterness, rage and anger, brawling and slander, along with every form of malice." (Ephesians 4:31)

▶ ***Resume*** your regular daily activities and social interaction with others. Look for ways to express love to others—and establish a "new normal."

Pray, "Lord, thank You for helping me reestablish my social life with those who are dear to me. Help me to receive their love, comfort, and support."

"Above all, love each other deeply, because love covers over a multitude of sins. Offer hospitality to one another without grumbling. Each one should use whatever gift he has received to serve others, faithfully administering God's grace in its various forms." (1 Peter 4:8–10)

SIGNIFICANCE

▶ *Realize* that your identity is in your relationship with the Lord and not in another person.

Pray, "Lord, thank You that my identity is not based on what others think about me, but that my true identity can be found only in a relationship with You."

"I have been crucified with Christ and I no longer live, but Christ lives in me. The life I live in the body, I live by faith in the Son of God, who loved me and gave himself for me." (Galatians 2:20)

▶ *Reflect* on the changes you made or lessons you learned as a result of being in the former relationship.

Pray, "Lord, thank You for all the lessons I learned from my past relationship. Thank You, Lord, for the growth that will continue to take place in my life."

"I applied my heart to what I observed and learned a lesson from what I saw." (Proverbs 24:32)

▶ *Reexamine* the strengths and weaknesses of the broken relationship and learn from any unwise decisions you made.

Pray, "Lord, thank You for wanting to develop discernment in me to help me see the unwise decisions I made while I was in the past relationship. Help me to overcome my weaknesses and grow in Your strength."

"The discerning heart seeks knowledge, but the mouth of a fool feeds on folly." (Proverbs 15:14)

▶ **Rehearse** instances that reflected sound judgment and discernment on your part.

Pray, "Lord, thank You for wanting to develop more and more sound judgment within me."

"My son, preserve sound judgment and discernment, do not let them out of your sight." (Proverbs 3:21)

▶ **Relegate** the past to the past and embrace your God-ordained future.

Pray, "Lord, thank You for helping me leave my past in the past and for preparing me to embrace my future with all that You have planned."

"Forget the former things; do not dwell on the past. See, I am doing a new thing! Now it springs up; do you not perceive it? I am making a way in the desert and streams in the wasteland." (Isaiah 43:18–19)

▶ **Reassure** your heart with the awareness that God has a perfect plan for your life.

Pray, "Lord, thank You that You are orchestrating Your plan for me even in the midst of heartbreaking circumstances."

"'I know the plans I have for you,' declares the LORD, 'plans to prosper you and not to harm you, plans to give you hope and a future.'" (Jeremiah 29:11)

SECURITY

▶ *Rest* in the sovereignty of God over all your plans and relationships.

Pray, "Lord, thank You for being sovereign in all areas of my life, including my relationships. Your plans for me are firmly set."

"The plans of the LORD stand firm forever, the purposes of his heart through all generations." (Psalm 33:11)

▶ *Relax* in the fact that God's plans and purposes for you cannot be thwarted by another person's actions.

Pray, "Lord, thank You that no circumstance and no person, including myself, can derail Your plans and purposes for me."

"I know that you can do all things; no plan of yours can be thwarted." (Job 42:2)

▶ *Remember* that God never allows anything in your life that He does not intend to use for your good.

Pray, "Lord, thank You that everything I experience in life will be used for my good, even the painful experiences will be used as a testimony to encourage others."

"We know that in all things God works for the good of those who love him, who have been called according to his purpose." (Romans 8:28)

▶ ***Resolve*** to face your heartache and to work through your grief with the Lord's help.

Pray, "Lord, thank You for being my Comforter and Counselor when I am faced with heartache and grief."

"He heals the brokenhearted and binds up their wounds." (Psalm 147:3)

▶ ***Resist*** the temptation to withdraw.

Pray, "Lord, thank You for wanting me to have meaningful relationships with others. Help me to seek the fellowship of friends and family even when I am tempted to withdraw."

"An unfriendly man pursues selfish ends; he defies all sound judgment." (Proverbs 18:1)

▶ ***Reaffirm*** your importance to God.

Pray, "Lord, thank You that You considered me important enough to create me, to make a plan for me, to die for me, and thank You for making a place for me in heaven."

"In my Father's house are many rooms; if it were not so, I would have told you. I am going there to prepare a place for you. And if I go and prepare a place for you, I will come back and take you to be with me that you also may be where I am." (John 14:2–3)

Your self-image has been shaped predominantly by the messages you received and internalized from others, from your experiences, and from your own self-talk. When you were a child, you did not have control over those in authority over you, but that is no longer the case. You are now able to choose those with whom you associate, and you can certainly control your self-talk. Therefore, you can take an active part in changing the distorted view you have of yourself by making a consistent effort to do the following:

▶ **Accept yourself.**

- Stop striving for perfection or to be like someone else.

- Realize that the Lord made you for a purpose, and He designed your personality and gave you the gifts and abilities He wanted you to have in order to accomplish His purpose for you.

"Many are the plans in a man's heart, but it is the Lord's purpose that prevails." (Proverbs 19:21)

▶ **Thank God for encouraging you.**

- Acknowledge and praise God for the abilities He has given you and for the things He has accomplished through you.

- Engage in biblically-based, encouraging self-talk and mute the condemning critic inside your head.

61

"May our Lord Jesus Christ himself and God our Father, who loved us and by his grace gave us eternal encouragement and good hope, encourage your hearts and strengthen you in every good deed and word." (2 Thessalonians 2:16–17)

▶ **Accept the compliments of others.**

- To discount the positive comments of those who have heartfelt appreciation for you is to discount their opinions and their desire to express their gratitude to you.

- Practice graciously accepting compliments and turning them into praise to God for the affirmation that He is at work in you and is producing good "fruit" through you.

"This is to my father's glory, that you bear much fruit, showing yourselves to be my disciples." (John 15:8)

▶ **Release past negative experiences and focus on a positive future.**

- Refuse to dwell on negative things said or done to you in the past and release them to God.

- Embrace the work God is doing in your life now and cooperate with Him by dwelling on Him and His character and His promises to you to fulfill His purposes in you.

"It is God who works in you to will and to act according to his good purpose." (Philippians 2:13)

▶ **Live in God's forgiveness.**

- Since God has extended to you forgiveness for all of your sins (past, present, and future), confess and repent of anything offensive to God. Do not set yourself up as a higher judge than God by refusing to forgive yourself.

- Lay harsh judgment of yourself aside and accept that you will not be made "fully perfect" and totally without sin until you stand in the presence of Christ and are fully conformed to His image.

"Dear friends, now we are children of God, and what we will be has not yet been made known. But we know that when he appears, we shall be like him, for we shall see him as he is. Everyone who has this hope in him purifies himself, just as he is pure." (1 John 3:2–3)

▶ **Benefit from mistakes.**

- Realize that you can learn from your mistakes as well as from the mistakes of others. Decide to view your mistakes as opportunities to learn needed lessons.

- Ask God what He wants to teach you from your mistakes, listen to Him and learn. Then move forward with a positive attitude and put into practice the insights you have gained.

"We know that in all things God works for the good of those who love him, who have been called according to his purpose." (Romans 8:28)

▶ Form supportive, positive relationships.

- Realize that critical people are hurt people who project their own feelings of inadequacy onto others in an attempt to ease their own emotional pain.

- Minimize the time you spend with negative, critical people—whether family, friends, or coworkers—and seek out those who encourage and support you both emotionally and spiritually.

"He who walks with the wise grows wise, but a companion of fools suffers harm." (Proverbs 13:20)

▶ Formulate realistic goals and plans.

- Solicit the help of others to identify your strengths, your weaknesses, the gifts God has given you, and the things you are persuaded God has called you to do.

- Prayerfully set some reasonable, achievable goals that capitalize on your strengths. Make a plan for how you will set about to accomplish those goals.

"Do you not know that in a race all the runners run, but only one gets the prize? Run in such a way as to get the prize." (1 Corinthians 9:24)

▶ Identify your heart's desires.

- Make a list of the things you have dreamed of doing but have never attempted because of a fear of failure or a lack of self-assurance.

- Share each desire with the Lord, asking Him to confirm to you which ones are from Him. Then lay out the steps you need to take in order to accomplish them.

"Delight yourself in the Lord and he will give you the desires of your heart." (Psalm 37:4)

▶ **Plan for success.**

- Anticipate any obstacles to accomplishing your goals and desires and plan strategies for overcoming them.
- Picture yourself achieving each of your goals and doing the things God has put on your heart to do.

"May he give you the desire of your heart and make all your plans succeed." (Psalm 20:4)

▶ **Celebrate each accomplishment.**

- Your feeling of self-worth and self-confidence will grow with the acknowledgement of each accomplishment.
- Rejoice with the Lord and other significant people over the things God and you have done together. Affirm and celebrate your success.

"There, in the presence of the Lord your God, you and your families shall eat and shall rejoice in everything you have put your hand to, because the Lord your God has blessed you." (Deuteronomy 12:7)

We all know the sickening feeling of living with a guilty conscience, or of knowing we have let others down, or of knowing we have let God down. One problem may be that we were not aiming at the right target. Like Samson in the book of Judges, we can be focused solely on self-gratification instead of on self-control. When we place ourselves in dependence upon God and when our target is right before God, we can have a clear conscience and can be a light in the midst of darkness.

> "I strive always to keep my conscience clear before God and man."
> (Acts 24:16)

Some sound spiritual reasons for having sexual integrity are ...

▶ "*I don't want* to do anything that will hinder my prayer life with God."

"If I had cherished sin in my heart, the LORD would not have listened." (Psalm 66:18)

▶ "*I want* God's blessing on my life."

"In view of God's mercy, to offer your bodies as living sacrifices, holy and pleasing to God—this is your spiritual act of worship." (Romans 12:1)

▶ "*I don't want* God's disfavor on the life of either of us."

"Do you not know that the wicked will not inherit the kingdom of God? Do not be deceived: Neither the sexually immoral nor idolaters nor adulterers nor male prostitutes nor homosexual offenders ... will inherit the kingdom of God." (1 Corinthians 6:9–10)

▶ "*I want* to live a life of integrity, being the same in the dark as I am in the light."

"I will not deny my integrity." (Job 27:5)

▶ "*I don't want* to take the place of God by trying to meet all the needs of another person."

"You shall have no other gods before me." (Deuteronomy 5:7)

▶ "*I want* others to see the power of Christ in me."

"His divine power has given us everything we need for life and godliness through our knowledge of him who called us by his own glory and goodness." (2 Peter 1:3)

▶ "*I don't want* anyone else to take the place of God in my life."

"Jesus replied: 'Love the Lord your God with all your heart and with all your soul and with all your mind.'" (Matthew 22:37)

Because *"I can do everything through him* [Christ] *who gives me strength"* (Philippians 4:13), I am closing the door to all thoughts of sexual involvement as a means of getting my needs met. The Lord will meet all of my needs.

> "My God will meet all your needs according to his glorious riches in Christ Jesus."
> (Philippians 4:19)

Invest in ...

INTEGRITY

Invite others to walk the road of sexual integrity with you.

- ▶ Allow yourself to be vulnerable with people whom you can trust.

- ▶ Share your struggle with a wise and understanding friend or mentor.

- ▶ Go to a spiritual leader or a support group and ask for accountability.

> *"Two are better than one, because they have a good return for their work: If one falls down, his friend can help him up. But pity the man who falls and has no one to help him up!"* (Ecclesiastes 4:9–10)

Never put yourself or your loved one in a tempting situation.

- ▶ Consider bedrooms off-limits.

- ▶ Don't be in a home alone with each other.

- ▶ Know your triggers—know what is sexually tempting to you and make a decision to counter those triggers.

> *"Do not offer the parts of your body to sin, as instruments of wickedness, but rather*

offer yourselves to God, as those who have been brought from death to life; and offer the parts of your body to him as instruments of righteousness." (Romans 6:13)

Trust God to meet your need for love.

▶ Don't use sexual pleasure to try to meet your needs for love and affirmation—it won't work!

▶ Learn to live in dependency upon the Lord. Give Him your heart.

▶ Let Him know that you are looking to Him to be your Need-Meeter.

"Let the morning bring me word of your unfailing love, for I have put my trust in you. Show me the way I should go, for to you I lift up my soul." (Psalm 143:8)

Enjoy others instead of using others.

▶ Don't try to fill up your "love bucket" with sex. Your bucket will have holes in it!

▶ Learn to be friends with each other—to enjoy doing many activities with each other.

▶ Realize that a real friend will never use you sexually.

"Love must be sincere. Hate what is evil; cling to what is good. Be devoted to one another in brotherly love. Honor one another above yourselves." (Romans 12:9–10)

Give yourself to only sexually pure relationships.

▶ Guard the gift of sexual intimacy until the time you are married.

▶ Keep the gift of sexual intimacy exclusively for your marriage partner.

▶ Realize that you can have an "intimate relationship" that is not a sexual relationship.

"Now that you have purified yourselves by obeying the truth so that you have sincere love for your brothers, love one another deeply, from the heart." (1 Peter 1:22)

Refuse to justify any sexual impurity.

▶ Honestly face the sexual sin in your life.

▶ Pray for God to convict you of any sin.

▶ Commit yourself to being a person of purity.

"Watch and pray so that you will not fall into temptation. The spirit is willing, but the body is weak." (Matthew 26:41)

Isolate yourself from people who tempt you.

▶ Leave any relationship that does not bring honor to God.

▶ Refuse to be with someone who dabbles in drugs or tries to use alcohol to weaken your will.

▶ State your commitment: "I will not allow myself to be alone with individuals who tempt me sexually."

"Do not be misled: 'Bad company corrupts good character.'" (1 Corinthians 15:33)

Transform your mind through the written Word of God.

▶ Find Scripture that is focused on your area of struggle.

▶ Ask God to reprogram your mind as you follow a discipline to read and memorize Scripture.

▶ Read one chapter of Proverbs daily.

"I have hidden your word in my heart that I might not sin against you." (Psalm 119:11)

Yield to Christ, who lives in you, trusting Him to produce in you a life of purity.

▶ Consciously submit your will to the will of Christ when you are tempted—do it *before* you are tempted.

▶ Don't lie to yourself—refuse to be lulled into false confidence in your own ability to withstand temptation.

▶ Live your life in dependence upon Christ, who lives within you. Jesus said,

"I am the true vine, and my Father is the gardener. He cuts off every branch in me that bears no fruit, while every branch that does

bear fruit he prunes so that it will be even more fruitful. You are already clean because of the word I have spoken to you. Remain in me, and I will remain in you. No branch can bear fruit by itself; it must remain in the vine. Neither can you bear fruit unless you remain in me. I am the vine; you are the branches. If a man remains in me and I in him, he will bear much fruit; apart from me you can do nothing." (John 15:1–5)

You can't be fulfilled in the way God intends unless you are connected to Him, living dependently on Him. If you allow Christ, who lives in you, to find expression through you, He will empower you to have sexual purity.

> **"Create in me a pure heart, O God, and renew a steadfast spirit within me." (Psalm 51:10)**

HOW TO Answer Common Questions

QUESTION: "What does undivided devotion to the Lord look like?"

ANSWER: To have undivided devotion to the Lord is ...

▶ To be wholly devoted to Him

▶ To be totally and completely committed to Him

▶ To rest the full weight of your personhood on Him

▶ To fully trust Him in every area of your life

▶ To seek to please Him in all you do

▶ To love Him with all your heart, soul, mind, and strength

Sitting in a chair or riding in an automobile or an airplane requires total commitment of yourself to the chair, the car, or the plane. To have undivided devotion to God requires ...

▶ Placing your entire life into God's hands

▶ Withholding nothing from God

▶ Allowing God to glorify Himself through you in all circumstances of life

▶ Giving God first place in your heart and life, making Him your master, ruler, and owner

▶ Obeying His commands and fully submitting to His will in your life

▶ Having no doubt regarding God, no reservation of mind, emotions, or will

The apostle James said,

"If any of you lacks wisdom, he should ask God, who gives generously to all without finding fault, and it will be given to him. But when he asks, he must believe and not doubt, because he who doubts is like a wave of the sea, blown and tossed by the wind. That man should not think he will receive anything from the Lord; he is a double-minded man, unstable in all he does."
(James 1:5–8)

QUESTION: "How can I develop undivided devotion to the Lord?"

ANSWER: To be devoted is to be committed. Therefore, to be devoted to God is to be committed to Him. Devotion to God is based on the worthiness of the character of God and the resulting righteous acts of God. It involves appraising the merits of God and making a decision to be committed to Him based on His merits.

Gaining an accurate understanding of God's character involves reading what is recorded in His Word about Him personally and about what He has done. And in your quest to know the character of God and have undivided devotion to Him, it will be beneficial for you to know the following things pertaining to His relationship to you:[9]

▶ **Know the reality of having your need for love satisfied in the depth of God's unconditional, everlasting love for you.**

- **Know that** God is the lover and supplier of your body and soul.

  *"I delight greatly in the LORD; my soul rejoices in my God. For he has clothed me with garments of salvation and arrayed me in a robe of righteousness, as a bridegroom adorns his head like a priest, and as a bride adorns herself with her jewels." (*Isaiah 61:10)

  *"Take my yoke upon you and learn from me, for I am gentle and humble in heart, and you will find rest for your souls." (*Matthew 11:29)

"Let the morning bring me word of your unfailing love, for I have put my trust in you. Show me the way I should go, for to you I lift up my soul." (Psalm 143:8)

- **Know that** each and every good thing in your life is a gift to you from your loving heavenly Father.

"Every good and perfect gift is from above, coming down from the Father of the heavenly lights, who does not change like shifting shadows." (James 1:17)

- **Know that** God made the whole of creation as an expression of His love toward you, to meet your needs, and for your enjoyment.

"God blessed them [Adam and Eve] and said to them, 'Be fruitful and increase in number; fill the earth and subdue it. Rule over the fish of the sea and the birds of the air and over every living creature that moves on the ground.' Then God said, 'I give you every seed-bearing plant on the face of the whole earth and every tree that has fruit with seed in it. They will be yours for food.'" (Genesis 1:28–29)

"Command those who are rich in this present world not to be arrogant nor to put their hope in wealth, which is so uncertain, but to put their hope in God, who richly provides us with everything for our enjoyment." (1 Timothy 6:17)

- **Know that** God has great compassion and tender concern toward all people, even those in rebellion against Him.

"God demonstrates his own love for us in this: While we were still sinners, Christ died for us. Since we have now been justified by his blood, how much more shall we be saved from God's wrath through him! For if, when we were God's enemies, we were reconciled to him through the death of his Son, how much more, having been reconciled, shall we be saved through his life!" (Romans 5:8–10)

- **Know that** the sacrifice of God's Son for your salvation was given out of His abounding love for you and for all people.

  "God so loved the world that he gave his one and only Son, that whoever believes in him shall not perish but have eternal life." (John 3:16)

▶ **Know the reality of having your need for significance satisfied in God's purposes for you.**

- **Know that** God is the source of your significance.

  "What is man that you are mindful of him, the son of man that you care for him? You made him a little lower than the heavenly beings and crowned him with glory and honor. You made him ruler over the works of your hands; you put everything under his feet." (Psalm 8:4–6)

- **Know that** God chose you to be His child, to bear His image, and to possess His life.

  "The Spirit himself testifies with our spirit that we are God's children." (Romans 8:16)

"God created man in his own image, in the image of God he created him; male and female he created them." (Genesis 1:27)

"When Christ, who is your life, appears, then you also will appear with him in glory." (Colossians 3:4)

- **Know that** God has selected you to be His messenger, His voice, His hands, His feet in order to show His heart, His character, and His plan of salvation to people throughout the world.

"Jesus came to them and said, 'All authority in heaven and on earth has been given to me. Therefore go and make disciples of all nations, baptizing them in the name of the Father and of the Son and of the Holy Spirit, and teaching them to obey everything I have commanded you. And surely I am with you always, to the very end of the age.'" (Matthew 28:18–20)

- **Know that** God has a specific plan and purpose for your life, a special reason for your being alive.

"'I know the plans I have for you,' declares the LORD, 'plans to prosper you and not to harm you, plans to give you hope and a future.'" (Jeremiah 29:11)

- **Know that** God delights in you, is glorified in you, and considers you His cherished possession, His priceless treasure.

"You also were included in Christ when you heard the word of truth, the gospel of your

salvation. Having believed, you were marked in him with a seal, the promised Holy Spirit, who is a deposit guaranteeing our inheritance until the redemption of those who are God's possession— to the praise of his glory." (Ephesians 1:13–14)

"Then those who feared the LORD talked with each other, and the LORD listened and heard. A scroll of remembrance was written in his presence concerning those who feared the LORD and honored his name. 'They will be mine,' says the LORD Almighty, 'in the day when I make up my treasured possession. I will spare them, just as in compassion a man spares his son who serves him.'" (Malachi 3:16–17)

▶ **Know the reality of having your need for security satisfied in your eternally secure relationship with God.**

- **Know that** God is the source of your security.

  "I give them eternal life, and they shall never perish; no one can snatch them out of my hand." (John 10:28)

- **Know that** God has entered into a covenant relationship with you, which is forever binding and cannot be broken.

  "This is my blood of the covenant, which is poured out for many for the forgiveness of sins." (Matthew 26:28)

- **Know that** God has placed you in Christ, that you are one with Him, and that you can never be separated from Him.

"My prayer is not for them alone. I pray also for those who will believe in me through their message, that all of them may be one, Father, just as you are in me and I am in you. May they also be in us so that the world may believe that you have sent me. I have given them the glory that you gave me, that they may be one as we are one: I in them and you in me. May they be brought to complete unity to let the world know that you sent me and have loved them even as you have loved me." (John 17:20–23)

- **Know that** God is sovereign over your life. Everything that touches you is first filtered through His fingers of love and is for your good.

  "We know that in all things God works for the good of those who love him, who have been called according to his purpose." (Romans 8:28)

- **Know that** God's Spirit surrounds you wherever you go, teaches you what you need to know, and holds you securely in the palm of His hand.

  "Where can I go from your Spirit? Where can I flee from your presence? If I go up to the heavens, you are there; if I make my bed in the depths, you are there. If I rise on the wings of the dawn, if I settle on the far side of the sea, even there your hand will guide me, your right hand will hold me fast" (Psalm 139:7–10).

  "My sheep listen to my voice; I know them, and they follow me. I give them eternal life, and they

shall never perish; no one can snatch them out of my hand. My Father, who has given them to me, is greater than all; no one can snatch them out of my Father's hand. I and the Father are one" (John 10:27–30).

To truly know God is to know that He is truly worthy of your undivided devotion.

> "You are worthy, our Lord and God,
> to receive glory and honor and power,
> for you created all things, and by your will
> they were created and have their being. ...
> And they sang a new song: 'You are worthy
> to take the scroll and to open its seals,
> because you were slain, and with your blood
> you purchased men for God from every tribe
> and language and people and nation.'"
> (Revelation 4:11; 5:9)

QUESTION: "How can I have an intimate relationship with God?"

ANSWER: Intimacy has been pronounced, "into me see" as a way of explaining what is involved in having an intimate relationship with someone. It is apparent that Jesus and His Father had the kind of relationship that enabled them to accurately see into the heart, soul, and mind of one another. Their relationship is a perfect model for us to follow in developing intimacy with God.

▶ Jesus deeply and wholeheartedly loved His Father.

▶ Jesus was totally devoted to His Father.

- Jesus sought to know the heart and mind of His Father.

- Jesus routinely spent time talking alone with His Father.

- Jesus listened to His Father.

- Jesus expressed His needs and desires to His Father.

- Jesus was united in purpose with His Father.

- Jesus' purpose in living was to reveal the heart and character of His Father.

- Jesus and the Father are mutually interdependent.

- Jesus drew His strength from His Father.

- Jesus was committed to doing the will of His Father.

- Jesus sought His Father's direction in all that He did.

- Jesus did everything He was told to do by His Father.

- Jesus performed good deeds to glorify His Father.

- Jesus and the Father are mutually submissive.

- Jesus entrusted Himself to His Father.

- Jesus willingly suffered to accomplish the will of His Father.

- Jesus pleased His Father rather than people.

> "A voice from heaven said, 'This is my Son,
> whom I love; with him I am well pleased.'"
> (Matthew 3:17)

QUESTION: "How do you reconcile singleness as being ordained by God for some people with what Moses wrote in Genesis 2:24, *'For this reason a man will leave his father and mother and be united to his wife, and they will become one flesh'*? Does this verse mean every man should marry?"

ANSWER: One key to the accurate interpretation of a particular Scripture is to remember that Scripture will never contradict Scripture. Therefore, it is imperative that the entire counsel of God (the entire Bible) be consulted when looking at a particular passage. Since there are several major people of faith (Jesus, the apostle Paul, Daniel, and others) whom God called to singleness, the proper interpretation of Genesis 2:24 is clearly not that every man should marry.

That being the case, what is another possibility for the meaning of this verse? One option is that God is simply making it clear to every man who desires to be sexually involved with a woman, that he must marry that woman. Further, marriage involves a man's leaving his home of origin—the home of his parents—being united in marriage with his wife, and then becoming one flesh with her through sexual intimacy. God is laying out the parameters for sexual encounters.

▶ He becomes united to his bride in the bonds of marriage.

▶ The groom establishes independence from his parents, evidenced by financial stability and emotional and spiritual maturity.

▶ He becomes one with her physically through sexual intercourse, consummating the marriage contract or vow.

▶ The "couple" is now husband and wife. They have become something different from what they were prior to exchanging their vows and entering into a binding, covenant, marriage relationship.

▶ They are now melded together into one new and different entity and can never go back (be separated) to what they individually were prior to becoming one.

"'At the beginning of creation God 'made them male and female.' 'For this reason a man will leave his father and mother and be united to his wife, and the two will become one flesh.' So they are no longer two, but one. Therefore what God has joined together, let man not separate."
(Mark 10:6–9)

QUESTION: "What about God's statement in Genesis 2:18: *'It is not good for the man to be alone. I will make a helper suitable for him'*? Doesn't this mean that it is not good for men to remain single?"

ANSWER: When God created all living *things*, He created them both male and female in order that they might multiply, with the result being, of course, that they were *not alone*. However, when it came to human beings, He first created the man Adam and placed him *alone* in the Garden of Eden. When God said that it was not good for the man (Adam) to be alone, the statement was made when he was the only human being in existence. God changed the man's status from being alone by giving him Eve, another human being—a female helper through whom he could multiply and fill the earth with offspring.

God clearly means for us to live in community—not to be alone. He created the biological family, the family of friends, and the spiritual family in which we are to individually live and grow into maturity. He clearly does not intend every man to marry in order *not to be alone*. No man has been *truly alone* since Adam.

"Two are better than one, because they have a good return for their work: If one falls down, his friend can help him up. But pity the man who falls and has no one to help him up!" (Ecclesiastes 4:9–10)

QUESTION: "I delight in the Lord, so why doesn't He give me the desire of my heart, which is to marry, as He promises in Psalm 37:4: *'Delight yourself in the LORD and he will give you the desires of your heart'*?"

ANSWER: This is a wonderful promise indeed, but the condition on which it is based is not necessarily understood without a grasp of the Hebrew meaning of "to delight" and "the desires of your heart."

▶ To *delight in the Lord* is to find extreme satisfaction, great pleasure, and keen enjoyment in Him. It is to find contentment in Him, to exult in Him, to relish time with Him, to be enraptured with Him, and to love and cherish Him.

▶ To *delight in the Lord* is to make Him our heart's delight. It is to find our solace and our rest in Him, to glory in who He is and in the knowledge that He is ours. It is to know His loving-kindness as our exceeding joy and deep satisfaction.

▶ The *desires of the heart* are the inclinations of a person's entire soul or self, not the appetites or longings of the body. The whole personality is involved in a person's desires.

▶ The *desires of a heart* that *delights in the Lord* are the deep cravings of a renewed and sanctified soul that is fully satisfied and totally content in Him.

▶ A heart that *delights in God* desires to know the love of God more thoroughly, to love God Himself more deeply, to understand His ways more clearly, and to please Him more extensively.

If the *desire of your heart* is selfish, you have not yet learned to *delight in the Lord*.

"Whom have I in heaven but you?
And earth has nothing I desire besides you."
(Psalm 73:25)

QUESTION: "How should I respond to people who keep telling me I need to be out there dating, when I am content being single?"

ANSWER: People may want you to be in a romantic relationship for any number of reasons.

Generally, they mean well. Try to guard against taking offense at their opinion. A safe response might be to tell them you appreciate their interest in you but you are really quite content in focusing on being the person God created you to be.

"Godliness with contentment is great gain."
(1 Timothy 6:6)

QUESTION: "How can anyone's worth be determined?"

ANSWER: At an auction, the worth of an item is determined clearly and simply by one thing: the highest price paid. Each item goes to the highest bidder. You were bought from the auction block of sin more than 2,000 years ago when the heavenly Father paid the highest price possible—the life of His Son, Jesus Christ. By that one act, your worth was forever established by God.

Jesus Christ paid the ultimate price for you—willingly dying on the cross—paying the penalty for your sins. He loves you that much!

Your true worth is based not on anything *you* have done or will do, but on what *Jesus has already done.* Without a doubt, He established your worth. You were worth His life. You were worth dying for.

> "Greater love has no one than this,
> that he lay down his life for his friends."
> (John 15:13)

HOW TO Realize Your Life Purpose

On April 9, 1945—just days before liberation by Allied Forces—Dietrich Bonhoeffer died at age 39, executed in Flossenburg at the Nazi concentration camp.

Frequently, Bonhoeffer had denounced "cheap" grace and, instead deemed it "costly." His summation: "It is costly because it costs a man his life, and it is grace because it gives a man the only true life."[10]

The old saying is true, "salvation is free" —but it is not cheap. It cost Jesus His life, and it costs you your life. When you become an authentic Christian, you yield control of your life to His control—then He takes control of your soul (your mind, will, and emotions).

Jesus put it all into perspective:

> "What good will it be for a man if he gains
> the whole world, yet forfeits his soul?"
> (Matthew 16:26)

When we allow the Lord to be Lord of our lives, He gives us His purpose. And then He gives us well-aimed goals to propel us to "reach the target"— to accomplish His purpose for our lives.

▶ **YOUR PURPOSE:** The *reason* for your life.

■ Purposes relate to the long-term *plan* God designed for you.

"In him we were also chosen, having been predestined according to the plan of him who works out everything in conformity with the purpose of his will." (Ephesians 1:11)

YOUR GOALS: The *routes* to reach your purpose.

■ Goals relate to the different types of work God leads you to do to accomplish your purpose.

"There are different kinds of service, but the same Lord. There are different kinds of working, but the same God works all of them in all men." (1 Corinthians 12:5–6)

▶ **YOUR PURPOSE:** The *why* of your life. (Why you are here on earth.)

■ Purposes relate to the *aim* of your life.

"Those God foreknew he also predestined to be conformed to the likeness of his Son." (Romans 8:29)

YOUR GOALS: The *what* of your life. (What you do on earth.)

■ Goals relate to the *activities* in your life.

"Be very careful, then, how you live—not as unwise but as wise, making the most of every opportunity ... Therefore do not be foolish, but understand what the Lord's will is." (Ephesians 5:15–17)

▶ **YOUR PURPOSE:** Establish *God's* target.

- Purposes are the *inspiration* behind your achievements.

  "Continue to work out your salvation with fear and trembling." (Philippians 2:12)

YOUR GOALS: *Measure* your movements to the target.

- Goals are the individual achievements.

  "You, O LORD, are loving. Surely you will reward each person according to what he has done." (Psalm 62:12)

▶ **YOUR PURPOSE:** Develop your life message.

- Purposes produce *inner* peace.

  "May the God of hope fill you with all joy and peace as you trust in him, so that you may overflow with hope by the power of the Holy Spirit." (Romans 15:13)

YOUR GOALS: Draw from your talents and abilities.

- Goals reveal *outer* progress.

  "Each one should use whatever gift he has received to serve others, faithfully administering God's grace in its various forms. If anyone speaks, he should do it as one speaking the very words of God. If anyone serves, he should do it with the strength God provides." (1 Peter 4:10–11)

PURPOSE

Bonhoeffer clearly knew and clung to God's purpose for him. As you seek God's purpose for your life ...

Picture your potential.

> **Ask:** "What vision does God have for me?"
>
> When God gives a vision, He also gives the provision.
>
> *"Where there is no vision, the people perish."* (Proverbs 29:18 KJV)

Use your failures as learning opportunities.

> **Ask:** "What am I learning?"
>
> *"It was good for me to be afflicted so that I might learn your decrees."* (Psalm 119:71)

Raise the bar.

> **Ask:** "How do I need to be stretched in order to grow as a person?"
>
> *"The one who calls you is faithful and he will do it."* (1 Thessalonians 5:24)

Persevere under trials.

> **Ask:** "In what areas am I growing because I am persevering?"
>
> *"Consider it pure joy, my brothers, whenever you face trials of many kinds, because you know that the testing of your faith develops perseverance.*

Perseverance must finish its work so that you may be mature and complete, not lacking anything." (James 1:2–4)

Open the doors to your options.

Ask: "What are the options I have not considered?"

"Trust in the LORD with all your heart and lean not on your own understanding; in all your ways acknowledge him, and he will make your paths straight." (Proverbs 3:5–6)

Serve from your heart.

Ask: "What does God want me to give to others?"

"It is more blessed to give than to receive." (Acts 20:35)

Eliminate your distractions.

Ask: "What is keeping me from doing what God wants me to do?"

"'Everything is permissible'—but not everything is beneficial. 'Everything is permissible'—but not everything is constructive." (1 Corinthians 10:23)

PRAYER OF PURPOSE

"Dear Heavenly Father,
I am amazed that You have a
unique plan and purpose for me!
How I thank You for wanting to be involved
in the most intimate details of my life.
It gives me tremendous hope to realize
that my entire life has meaning and that
You can accomplish Your purposes
no matter what I have or haven't done.
I ask that You reveal Your purposes
for my life as I study Your Word
and pray for Your leading.
Help me discover Your specific goals
and plans for my life in order to fulfill those
purposes. Thank You, Father,
that You know the true desires of my heart
and that You will work in my life
to accomplish my reason for living!
In Jesus' name. Amen."

If you are single, for whatever length
of time, your purposeful God has a plan
to use this time powerfully in your life.
Don't miss the beauty of now!
God is nurturing the soil of your life so that
you can bring beauty to the lives of others.
Bloom where you are planted now!

—June Hunt

SCRIPTURES TO MEMORIZE

Without a mate, I don't see any purpose for my life.

"The LORD will fulfill his purpose for me; your love, O LORD, endures forever." (Psalm 138:8)

Will I be content if I find someone to marry?

"I have learned to be content whatever the circumstances." (Philippians 4:11)

I don't feel complete or fulfilled without a mate.

"In Christ all the fullness of the Deity lives in bodily form, and you have been given fullness in Christ, who is the head over every power and authority." (Colossians 2:9–10)

I'm often very lonely without a life companion. Is God near me?

"Come near to God and he will come near to you." (James 4:8)

I'm really afraid of growing old alone.

"Surely I am with you always, to the very end of the age." (Matthew 28:20)

How can I live without someone special to love?

"Live in a right way in undivided devotion to the Lord." (1 Corinthians 7:35)

I'm not sure I'll be able to live a sex-free life.

"I can do everything through him who gives me strength." (Philippians 4:13)

I must do all I can to meet potential marriage partners.

"I know, O LORD, that a man's life is not his own; it is not for man to direct his steps." (Jeremiah 10:23)

Why hasn't God brought a mate to me?

"For your Maker is your husband—the LORD Almighty is his name—the Holy One of Israel is your Redeemer; he is called the God of all the earth." (Isaiah 54:5)

Is it wrong for me to pray for a mate?

"Do not be anxious about anything, but in everything, by prayer and petition, with thanksgiving, present your requests to God." (Philippians 4:6)

NOTES

1. *Merriam-Webster Collegiate Dictionary*, s.v. "Single"; http://www.m-w.com.

2. *Merriam-Webster*, s.v. "Single"

3. James Strong, *Strong's Hebrew Lexicon* (electronic edition; Online Bible Millennium Edition v. 1.13) (Timnathserah Inc., July 6, 2002).

4. Davis and Denney, *The Healing Choice*, (Waco: Word Books, 1986), 78.

5. Gary R. Collins, *Christian Counseling: A Comprehensive Guide*, rev. ed., (Dallas: Word, 1988), 366–368.

6. Collins, *Christian Counseling*, 363–365.

7. Lawrence J. Crabb, Jr., *Understanding People: Deep Longings for Relationship*, Ministry Resources Library (Grand Rapids: Zondervan, 1987), 15–16; Robert S. McGee, *The Search for Significance*, 2nd ed. (Houston, TX: Rapha, 1990), 27–30.

8. Crabb, Jr., *Understanding People*, 15–16; McGee, *The Search for Significance*, 27–30.

9. Crabb, Jr., *Understanding People*, 15–16; McGee, *The Search for Significance*, 27–30.

10. Deitrich Bonhoeffer, *The Cost of Discipleship*, (New York: MacMillan, 1963), 47.

June Hunt's HOPE FOR THE HEART minibooks are biblically-based, and full of practical advice that is relevant, spiritually-fulfilling and wholesome.

HOPE FOR THE HEART TITLES

www.aspirepress.com